# 25 Projects for eco Explorers

# 25 Projects for eco Explorers

## CHRISTINE M. KIRKER

ALA Editions

CHICAGO | 2020

ISBN: 978-0-8389-4751-7

**Library of Congress Cataloging-in-Publication Data**

Names: Kirker, Christine M., 1970- author.

Title: 25 projects for eco explorers / Christine M. Kirker.

Other titles: Twenty-five projects for eco explorers

Description: Chicago : ALA Editions, 2020. | Includes bibliographical references. | Summary: "Designed for kids aged 4-10, and flexible enough to use in either story-times or classroom settings, the projects included introduce kids to many of the current environmental topics in our world. Each topic will be presented through the lens of a representative picture book, then further enhanced with detailed information and reinforced with a hands-on project"—Provided by publisher.

Identifiers: LCCN 2020000767 | ISBN 9780838947517 (paperback)

Subjects: LCSH: Elementary school libraries—Activity programs—United States. | School librarian participation in curriculum planning—United States. | Environmental sciences—Study and teaching (Elementary)—Activity programs. | Environmental sciences—Juvenile literature—Bibliography.

Classification: LCC Z675.S3 K54 2020 | DDC 027.8/222—dc23

LC record available at https://lccn.loc.gov/2020000767

Book design by Kim Thornton in the Cardea and the Vista Slab typefaces.
Cover images © Adobe Stock.

♾ This paper meets the requirements of ANSI/NISO Z39.48-1992 (Permanence of Paper).

Printed in the United States of America

24 23 22 21 20    5 4 3 2 1

**FOR ASHLEIGH AND SEAN**
*and the hope for a brighter tomorrow.*

# Contents

# Introduction

INCREASINGLY OUR NEWS IS FILLED WITH REPORTS OF CLIMATE CHANGE, SEVERE weather, and melting polar ice caps. How do these topics affect us, especially when they seem to be abstract concepts that may not directly influence our daily lives? Even when we understand the issues, they seem so large that we often wonder what we can do to help generate change. *25 Projects for Eco Explorers* aims to introduce students to many of the current environmental topics in our world. Often teachers are uncertain how to incorporate these topics into their current curriculum. *25 Projects for Eco Explorers* will explore 25 environmental topics and demonstrate how they can be integrated into K-5 educational lesson plans and programming for children aged 4-10.

Each chapter will be introduced through a relevant picture book that will help explain the importance of the environmental topic. Detailed information about the topic will be presented, along with Learn More and Did You Know sections that explore interesting related facts. A hands-on project is included to help reinforce learning. All chapters can be simplified or expanded to fit the age group you are working with. While I use the term students often through the text, I am referring to all young learners in a variety of educational settings. My hope is that *25 Projects for Eco Explorers* is a launching point for programming that is relatable to today's issues.

# Honeybees

### *The Honeybee*

Kirsten Hall. Illustrated by Isabelle Arsenault. New York, NY: Atheneum Books for Young Readers, 2018.

Spring is the perfect time to teach kids about honeybees since this is the season that they awaken! In spring, flowers bloom and honeybees get their fill of pollen and nectar. With a wiggle and a waggle, they show their fellow honeybees where they can find the best flowers for nectar to bring back to the hive. Then the magic happens—they take the nectar and flap their wings until honey is finally made. Honeybees are not only essential for providing honey, but also for contributing to the pollination of many of the fruits and vegetables we consume. A wonderful introduction to honeybees, this book explains how each season influences honeybees' routines. Illustrations enhance the story with gentle hints to show what each season offers.

### ABOUT HONEYBEES

Honeybees live in colonies within hives. As honeybees travel from plant to plant looking for nectar, they spread pollen, which causes seeds to form. Honeybees communicate inside the hive by using either the round dance or waggle dance. When a honeybee does the round dance, she is telling the other bees that the flowers are close to the hive. The dancing bee walks in a circle then turns and goes the other way, alerting the bees to go outside and fly in a circular pattern near the hive until they find the flowers. When a honeybee does the waggle dance, she walks around in two loops and shakes her body. The angle of the dance indicates the direction of the flowers. The dance also tells them how far away the flowers are. The longer a bee dances for, the further away the flowers are from the hive. During the dance, the bee will pause and give samples of the nectar she gathered to the other bees. Bees can also smell with their antennae the sweet scent of flowers they visited. If the dancing bee buzzes loudly and performs the dance vigorously, the other bees become excited too.

### BOOKS TO DISPLAY

*Bee Dance* by Rick Chrustowski. New York, NY: Henry Holt and Co., 2015.

*The Buzz on Bees: Why Are They Disappearing?* by Shelley Rotner and Anne Woodhull. New York, NY: Holiday House, 2010.

*How Do Bees Make Honey?* by Melissa Stewart. New York, NY: Marshall Cavendish Benchmark, 2009.

# Hands-on Project

After reading the book *Bee Dance* by Rick Chrustowski, have kids practice their own waggle dance. The role of a scout honeybee is to discover new food sources, meaning flowers that provide pollen. The scout collects all the pollen she can carry, then takes it back to the hive and tells the other bees where to find it. A honeybee scout can choose to either do the round dance or the waggle dance depending on where the flowers are located. For flowers more than 100 yards away from the hive, she performs the waggle dance. See how well the students can interpret the dance moves of the scout. Remember, when a scout honeybee finds a good batch of flowers, she tells the hive and other forager bees where she found them through her dance.

## MATERIALS NEEDED

- Artificial or real flowers, or a photo of flowers

## DIRECTIONS

1. Decide on a location to hide the flowers. Have one student be the scout honeybee who will instruct the others where the flowers are located.

2. The waggle dance is performed as a figure eight or two side-by-side halves. The number of waggles tells the other bees how far the flowers are. If flowers are nearby, perform the waggle dance once. If flowers are far away, perform the waggle dance two or three times.

3. Have the scout face the direction of the flowers and have the scout follow the instructions below to perform the waggle dance.

Waggle your bottom while walking a few steps. Circle to the right and return to the starting point. Waggle up the center again, and then circle to the left and return to the starting point. That is one complete waggle dance. Do this as often as needed to demonstrate the distance of the flowers.

4. When the scout stops dancing, have the other students travel in the direction the scout indicated and begin searching for the flowers.

5. Have the students take turns hiding the flowers, being the scout bee, and performing the waggle dance.

**LEARN MORE** Life in a honeybee hive is very organized, with each bee performing a role to support the community it lives in. Queen bees and drones have important roles, but most of the work is done by the worker bees, which are the smallest bees in the hive. They are female workers and their chores include making honey, cleaning the hive, guarding the colony, and cleaning and feeding the queen, drones, and larva. In addition, they are responsible for building the wax combs and visiting the flowers. They are truly workers! Think about your role in your family, classroom and neighborhood. What responsibilities do you have that help the community? What chores do you have that help contribute to your home running smoothly? How do these tasks relate to the bees' community?

# Monarch Butterflies

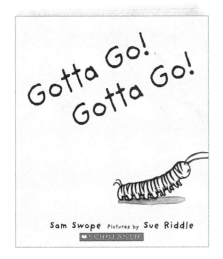

### *Gotta Go! Gotta Go!*

Sam Swope. New York, NY: Farrar, Straus and Giroux, 2000.

In this classic tale, an egg becomes a caterpillar who knew it had to go to Mexico. This story teaches kids how caterpillars transform into butterflies and explores the journey that monarch butterflies take as they migrate south. The caterpillar crawls and eats, and eats and crawls, but eventually becomes too tired to crawl any further. After sleeping for days, the caterpillar transforms into something new—a monarch butterfly! The butterfly begins to fly as fast as it can to Mexico, where it can dance with other monarchs. Eventually though, monarchs must return home, so they can lay new eggs and begin the cycle again.

### ABOUT MONARCH BUTTERFLIES

Monarch butterflies have a distinctive orange and black pattern that is easily recognizable. Monarchs start as an egg, often found on thick green leaves of a milkweed plant. The egg then turns into a caterpillar that eats the leaves of the milkweed. This is the only type of leaf that monarchs eat; the leaf contains a chemical that makes the caterpillars taste bad to predators. After about two weeks, caterpillars attach themselves to a branch and curl into a J shape. The caterpillar forms a chrysalis that sparkles like a green jewel with a golden thread. About nine days after that, the chrysalis darkens and cracks, and a monarch butterfly emerges. After drying its wings, the butterfly drinks nectar from flowers to begin to store energy for its long journey. In the fall, monarchs from the northern and eastern parts of the United States fly to Mexico. Those from western states fly to California. Migrating monarchs travel 50–100 miles per day and can travel up to 3,000 miles during migration.

According to the National Wildlife Federation, the monarch population is in decline, as they are experiencing habitat loss and their migration is being affected by changes in climate. Once plentiful, milkweed is now less common because of increasing urban and agricultural development and the widespread use of herbicides. Without

### BOOKS TO DISPLAY

*A Monarch Butterfly's Journey* by Suzanne Slade. Mankato, MN: Picture Window Books, 2012.

*The Monarchs Are Missing: A Butterfly Mystery* by Rebecca E. Hirsch. Minneapolis, MN: Millbrook Press, 2018.

*Señorita Mariposa* by Ben Gundersheimer. New York, NY: Nancy Paulsen Books, 2019.

frequent resting spots where there is milkweed, monarchs are unable to make the long migration journey. Furthermore, herbicides and pesticides not only destroy milkweed, but can make surviving milkweed plants toxic.

### DID YOU KNOW?

No single migrating monarch butterfly makes the whole round trip. Typically one "super generation" makes the journey south, while it takes three or four generations to complete the trip north. Southern migrating monarchs live longer and travel further. They also help the planet as they migrate by pollinating wildflowers. Once the monarchs reach the Sierra Madre mountains in Mexico, they will hibernate together in the oyamel fir trees.

## Hands-on Project

Monarch butterflies rely on their wings to migrate to Mexico. Have participants use their engineering skills to create a butterfly with moveable wings from a variety of available items.

### MATERIALS NEEDED

- Brad fasteners
- Glue
- Tape
- Scissors
- A variety of paper including recycled newspapers, books, and magazines
- Pipe cleaners
- Paper egg cartons
- Buttons, googly eyes, and stickers to decorate
- Markers or crayons

### DIRECTIONS

Have participants follow the instructions below to create their own butterfly.

1. Using a variety of items, have participants construct a butterfly. The butterfly can be any size, but the wings must be able to move.

2. Explain how butterflies have symmetrical patterns on each wing, and then have participants decorate the wings of their butterflies with symmetrical patterns.

**LEARN MORE** An easy way to help the monarch butterflies on their journey is to create a monarch waystation, a garden that provides food for monarch butterflies. Whether at home or school, adding milkweeds and other nectar plants can make a positive impact on their habitat. For more information in creating and registering your site as a monarch waystation, visit **monarchwatch.org/waystations**.

# Pollinators

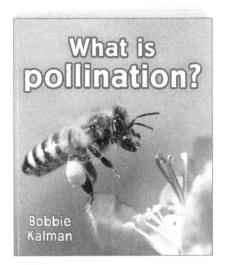

## *What Is Pollination?*

Bobbie Kalman. New York, NY: Crabtree Publications, 2011.

This informative book discusses all aspects of pollination, from parts of the plant to the many pollinators that help make our food. Pollination is responsible for much of our food production, and this book helps kids learn about the insects and animals that pollinate so that they can better understand pollinators' significance to our ecosystem. Colorful photographs enhance the text and help readers realize how important it is to protect the habitat of these creatures.

### ABOUT POLLINATORS

Pollen is a part of the flower that plants need to make fruit, seeds, and new plants. Pollen needs to move from one flower to another of the same kind of flower to make new plants. While some flowers can self-pollinate, most flowers need pollinators to move their pollen, which is called cross pollination. Pollinators include bees, wasps, butterflies, and other small insects and animals, such as birds and bats that visit flowers. Insects and animals pollinate when they are looking for nectar to eat. After a flower is pollinated, its petals fall off. Some parts of the flowers become fruits or vegetables; others become seeds. More than one third of the food we eat depends on pollinators.

### DID YOU KNOW?

There are thousands of insects that pollinate plants, including bees, wasps, butterflies, moths, and flies. Bees collect nectar and pollen from flowers and pollinate many kinds of fruits and vegetables. Honeybees also make honey that we can eat. Butterflies and moths have a long proboscis, a tubular feeding mechanism like a straw, that can reach nectar and pollen inside flowers. Wasps visit flowers to look for smaller insects that they eat. While hunting insects, wasps pollinate plants by carrying pollen on their

**BOOKS TO DISPLAY**

*Experiment with Pollination* by Nadia Higgins. Minneapolis, MN: Lerner Publications Co., 2015.

*Insect Pollinators* by Jennifer Boothroyd. Minneapolis, MN: Lerner Publications Co., 2015.

*What if There Were No Bees? A Book About the Grassland Ecosystem* by Suzanne Slade. Mankato, MN: Picture Window Books, 2011.

bodies from flower to flower. There are also many species of flies that visit flowers to drink nectar. While looking for smaller insects to eat, beetles carry the nectar from the flowers on their bodies. Birds around the world feed on nectar or insects found in flowers as well. Their beaks are specially adapted to reach the nectar allowing the sticky grains of pollen to cling to them. Other small animals also pollinate plants. Lizards, fruit bats, and honey possums all use their long snout and tongue to reach inside the flower to eat nectar and pollen.

# Hands-on Project

Have students create and drop seed bombs to grow flowers and see which pollinators are attracted to the flowers that grow. Toss your seed bomb at home, an open field, or at an approved restoration area.

## MATERIALS NEEDED

- Air-dry clay
- Potting soil
- Packet of flower seeds, or a mixture of seeds of your choosing
- Rolling pin
- Butter or plastic knife

## DIRECTIONS

Have participants follow the instructions below to create their own seed bombs.

1. Break off a piece of clay about the size of your fist and roll it out flat.

2. Sprinkle some potting soil on the clay, leaving an edge of clay visible.

3. Sprinkle some seeds on top of the soil.

4. Grab the visible edge of clay and fold the clay over the soil.

5. Slowly knead the clay, incorporating the soil and seeds within the clay.

6. Roll the clay into a long log.

7. Using a knife, cut the log into smaller pieces and roll them into balls.

8. Let the balls dry outside in the sun or in a sunny spot inside.

9. When the seed balls are dry, have students take their seed bombs to toss and start their wildflower garden.

**LEARN MORE** NOVA provides a pollination game, which includes a printable version, to match seven plants with their pollinators. To play the game and learn more about pollinators, visit **pbs.org/wgbh/nova/nature/pollination-game.html.**

# Loggerhead Turtles

### *Follow the Moon Home*

Philippe Cousteau, Jr. and Deborah Hopkinson. San Francisco, California: Chronicle Books, 2016.

When a girl moves to a new town, she discovers that baby loggerhead sea turtles can get confused trying to find the ocean after they hatch. At night, the turtles follow the bright lights of beach houses instead of turning toward the moonlit sea. Soon she and her classmates create a plan to save the turtles by getting the town to turn off their lights at night. Great for kids aged 4-8, this book empowers children to be active explorers and change agents, teaching them that anyone can make a difference in the world.

### ABOUT LOGGERHEAD TURTLES

Loggerhead sea turtles are found in the Atlantic, Pacific, and Indian Oceans. While they are the most abundant sea turtle in U.S. coastal waters, nesting from North Carolina to Florida, they are endangered throughout the world. From May to mid-August, loggerhead turtle mothers come to shore to dig their nests and lay their eggs. Each female turtle lays an average of 120 eggs per season and eggs typically hatch in 55-60 days, from July to the end of October. On land, beach development and artificial lighting threaten loggerhead nests and hatchlings. Once hatched, baby turtles instinctively follow the brightest light, ideally the moon over water, making it to the ocean. However, the bright lights of nearby homes and businesses can make the hatchlings turn inland instead. For those that safely make it back to the ocean, they have to worry about fishing gear, such as longlines and nets, along with garbage in the ocean that threaten their habitat. Loggerhead turtles are protected under the Endangered Species Act and many conservationist groups are working to ensure their recovery and survival. They are essential to the marine ecosystem, as they help maintain coral reefs and marine sea grasses.

### BOOKS TO DISPLAY

*Mission Sea Turtle Rescue: All About Sea Turtles and How to Save Them* by Karen Romano Young. Washington, DC: National Geographic, 2015.

*Ocean Commotion: Sea Turtles* by Janeen Mason. Gretna, LA: Pelican Publishing Co., 2006.

*Turtle Summer: A Journal for My Daughter* by Mary Alice Monroe. Mount Pleasant, SC: Sylvan Dell Pub., 2007.

# Hands-on Project

Turtles are a favorite animal throughout the world. Have students create their own turtle with a mosaic shell.

## MATERIALS NEEDED

- Sea turtle image like the one shown
- Card stock
- Scissors
- Tissue paper
- Colored pencils
- Contact paper

## DIRECTIONS

Copy and print a turtle image using the one provided, or one of your choosing, on card stock for each student. Then have participants follow the directions below to create their own faux stained-glass sea turtle.

1. Carefully cut out the shell portion of the turtle. (If students are too young, or time is an issue, precut the pieces for your class.)

2. Cut an assortment of colored tissue paper into smaller shapes.

3. On the backside of the card stock turtle, place a piece of contact paper.

4. Create a mosaic shell by placing the colored tissue on the sticky contact paper. Think about a pattern you may want to create, and how many scales you want your turtle to have.

5. When complete, place another piece of contact paper over the top of the turtle. Placing the turtle near a window where light will shine through will create a stained-glass effect.

### DID YOU KNOW?

A female loggerhead turtle will only lay eggs on the beach where she hatched. Adult females typically reach maturity after 35 years and will travel up to 12,000 kilometers every two to three years to their nesting grounds. Turtles usually hatch at night when the sand is cooler.

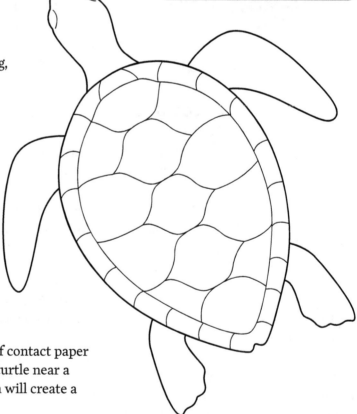

Source: © olkita/Adobe Stock, https://stock.adobe.com/247825874.

**LEARN MORE** To learn more about the life cycle of a sea turtle, visit **nwf.org/ Educational-Resources/Wildlife-Guide/Reptiles/Sea-Turtles/Loggerhead-Sea-Turtle.**

# Mountain Gorillas

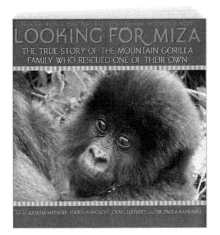

### *Looking for Miza: The True Story of the Mountain Gorilla Family Who Rescued One of Their Own*

Juliana Hatkoff, Isabella Hatkoff, Craig Hatkoff, and Dr. Paula Kahumbu. New York, NY: Scholastic Press, 2008.

Nearly 400 mountain gorillas make their home in the jungles of Virunga National Park, located in the Democratic Republic of Congo in Africa. This is over half of the planet's remaining mountain gorilla population. The park is monitored by rangers who visit the area each day and lead tourists safely into the jungle. The rangers not only track the mountain gorillas, but they also try to protect them from poachers. *Looking for Miza* tells the story of a young gorilla that was lost in the forest, and Miza's silverback father, Kabirizi, who found her. Great for readers aged 7-10, this book provides interesting details about the mountain gorillas' habitat, their group behaviors, and the area in the Congo where they live.

### ABOUT MOUNTAIN GORILLAS

Mountain gorillas live in family groups called troops. Each troop is led by a strong male, called a silverback. The gorillas eat leaves, stems, fruit, seeds, and roots. Adult male mountain gorillas eat up to 60 pounds of food per day and grow to 4-6 feet in length. Baby gorillas stay with their mothers until they are between 4-6 years old, and the mothers often nurse until the babies are three. Mountain gorillas live in elevations of 8,000 to 13,000 feet. They have thick fur, which helps them stay warm in the colder mountain temperatures.

Despite efforts to protect animals around the world, mountain gorillas remain endangered. It is estimated that there are about 1,000 mountain gorillas left on earth. Virunga National Park is the natural habitat for the largest concentration of mountain gorillas, with an estimated 60 percent of the population living there. However, the Democratic Republic of Congo and its neighboring countries in Africa suffer from ethnic conflicts and unstable political situations. Many displaced people seek refuge in camps at the base of the mountains,

**BOOKS TO DISPLAY**

*Actual Size* by Steve Jenkins. New York, NY: Houghton Mifflin Harcourt, 2004.

*Don't Let Them Disappear: 12 Endangered Species Across the Globe* by Chelsea Clinton. New York, NY: Philomel Books, 2019.

*Face to Face with Gorillas* by Michael Nichols and Elizabeth Carney. Washington, DC: National Geographic, 2009.

*I Am Jane Goodall* by Brad Meltzer. New York, NY: Dial Books for Young Readers, 2016.

*The Watcher: Jane Goodall's Life with the Chimps* by Jeanette Winter. New York, NY: Schwartz and Wade Books, 2011.

destroying forests that are part of the gorillas' natural habitat and leaving them without the natural resources they need for survival. Other dangers to the gorillas come from poachers who hunt them and from diseases that they can contract from human visitors to the area.

### DID YOU KNOW?

In 1960, Jane Goodall traveled from England to the Gombe Stream National Park in Western Tanzania to study chimps. With time and patience, she accumulated a wealth of information about chimpanzees' patterns of behavior that she shared with the world. Jane Goodall has spent her life as an outspoken advocate for the chimpanzees and called for the protection of their habitat. To learn more about Jane Goodall's work, visit **https://www.janegoodall.org/our-story/about-jane.**

# Hands-on Project

In his engaging book *Actual Size*, Steve Jenkins shows the actual size of animals. Using measuring sticks and the book *Actual Size*, or life-size drawings, have students compare measurements of themselves to the size of a gorilla and other animals.

## MATERIALS NEEDED

- *Actual Size* by Steve Jenkins or look up animal sizes/body parts of interest on the internet and have those measurements handy
- Measuring tape, yard stick, ruler
- Pencil
- Paper

## DIRECTIONS

Have participants follow the directions below to compare their size to that of other animals.

1. Measure your height and make note of it.

2. Measure your hand length from your wrist to your longest finger and make note of it.

3. Measure your foot length and make note of it.

4. Compare your measurements to the size of various animals of interest.

**LEARN MORE** Virunga National Park was designated a UNESCO World Heritage Site in 1979. The Virunga Mountains are a range of extinct volcanoes that border the Democratic Republic of Congo, Rwanda, and Uganda. The park has bubbling lava lakes, savannah plains, and dense jungles. The savannah is home to wildlife, including elephants, lions, hippos, and buffalo. The mountain gorillas live on the forested slopes of the Park's volcanoes. To see the mountain gorillas in their natural habitat, visit **youtube.com/watch?v=QyCAVHRiUKs.**

# Polar Bears

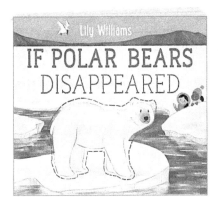

## *If Polar Bears Disappeared*

Lily Williams. New York, NY: Roaring Brook Press, 2018.

Covering the difficult but important topic of climate change, *If Polar Bears Disappeared* provides an overview of the interconnectedness of the warming climate, melting ice, and the animals dependent on one another for survival, including polar bears, ringed seals, and orcas. Polar bears are an endangered species in fear of extinction, and this book explores what will happen if the Arctic sea ice continues to melt and polar bears go extinct. This thoughtful and engaging text makes a complex topic approachable for young readers and explains how the loss of one species can cause damaging effects to the world's ecosystem.

### ABOUT POLAR BEARS

Polar bears are the largest land predators on earth. Male bears weigh over 1,000 pounds and can grow up to 11 feet long. Females can weigh over 700 pounds and can grow up to 8 feet long. During one meal alone, they can eat up to 100 pounds of meat. Even with their enormous size, they can run up to 26 miles per hour for short distances and can swim up to 60 miles without resting. They have an amazing sense of smell that helps them detect seals from miles away. Polar bear fur is not actually white—it is made up of clear hollow tubes of hair that reflect light and make the bears look white. Their fur can also quickly shed water after the bears swim, which helps keep them warm. Polar bear skin is actually black, which helps them absorb the sun's rays and keep them warm. They also have a four-inch layer of fat under their skin that insulates their body. As the Earth continues to warm, the arctic sea ice continues to melt. Polar bears use sea ice for platforms when they hunt for seals. When the ice melts, the polar bears have to stop feeding and move to shore. With ice melting earlier each year, polar bears are not able to pack on as much weight, leading to fewer and weaker cubs.

### BOOKS TO DISPLAY

*The Magic School Bus and the Climate Challenge* by Joanna Cole. New York, NY: Scholastic Press, 2010.

*Polar Bear, Why Is Your World Melting?* by Robert E. Wells. Morton Grove, Ill.: Albert Whitman & Co., 2008.

*Vanishing Ice* by Robert Coupe. New York, NY: PowerKids Press, 2013.

*Winston of Churchill: One Bear's Battle Against Global Warming* by Jean Davies Okimoto. Seattle, WA: Sasquatch Books, 2007.

### DID YOU KNOW?

The polar ice cap reaches about 500 miles down from the North Pole with the Arctic Circle encompassing an imaginary circular area around the North Pole. It includes the Arctic Ocean and northern parts of Alaska, Canada, Russia, Norway, Sweden, Finland, and most of Greenland. Many parts of the Arctic are flat and bare; these areas are known as the Arctic tundra. Much of the soil in the tundra stays frozen all year; this phenomenon is called permafrost. Other parts of the Arctic have tall mountains, lakes, and rivers. The area closest to the North Pole is called the High Arctic and is the coldest part of the Arctic Circle. It has poor soil and few animals live there. The Low Arctic is the farthest from the North Pole. Plants in the Low Arctic cover much of the land and can support many animals. The Arctic is about 29 degrees below zero (Fahrenheit) in its coldest months of January and February. Climate change is causing the polar ice caps to melt at an alarming rate. Human activities, such as burning fossil fuels, cause the planet to warm up and melt the polar ice. Melting ice is not only a problem for arctic animals, it is also a larger problem for the planet, as melting ice is essential to reflect the sun's rays to help keep the planet from overheating. Additionally, melting ice causes sea levels to rise, flooding many low-lying communities.

# Hands-on Project

This project demonstrates how ice can melt at different rates.

### MATERIALS NEEDED

- Three aluminum small pie plates per child, each filled with water and frozen overnight
- Three small, 5 oz paper cups per child
- Water
- Teaspoon
- Salt
- Magnifying glasses

### DIRECTIONS

#### The Day Before the Planned Activity

Fill enough small pie plates with water so that each child for the activity will have three small plates. Place in the freezer to freeze overnight.

> **LEARN MORE** For two months in the summer, the sun doesn't set in the Arctic. It shines for 24 hours a day, giving the area the nickname the Land of the Midnight Sun. As the Earth travels around the sun, it slowly begins to tip toward the sun in the summer, then tilt away in the winter.

#### Day of Activity

1. Fill one small paper cup per child with cool water.
2. Fill one small paper cup per child with a teaspoon of salt.
3. Fill one small paper cup per child with a teaspoon of salt and water.
4. Give each child three aluminum plates with frozen ice and a cup with each of the different melting solutions and have participants follow the directions below to see how different variables affect ice melting.

   - Try a different melting solution on each plate of ice.
   - Observe and describe what happened with each of the melting solutions. Which solution melted the ice first? Which made a hole through the center? Which caused cracks?

#### Explaining the Results of the Activity

Salt lowers the freezing point of water. When students sprinkle salt directly on ice, they should notice that it will melt the ice on contact and create cracks and craters. Saltwater raises the freezing point of ice and will melt a concentrated area quickly.

# Protecting Endangered Animals

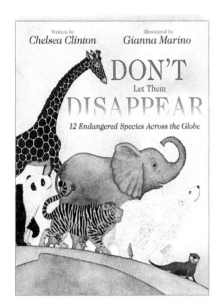

## Don't Let Them Disappear: 12 Endangered Species Across the Globe

Chelsea Clinton. New York, NY: Philomel Books, 2019.

Twelve endangered animals, including pandas, sea otters, and whales, are featured in this book, which describes how these animals spend their days. Their unique characteristics are shared, as well as their habitat and endangered status. Focusing on these familiar, lovable animals allows young readers a better understanding of what extinction could mean for our world. Overall risks to animals are discussed, along with suggestions on what we can do to help keep these animals on our planet.

## ABOUT ENDANGERED AND EXTINCT CLASSIFICATIONS

Scientists at the International Union for Conservation of Nature have developed a classification system to measure the extinction risk of animal species. *Extinction* means that no animals of that species remain on Earth, while *extinct in the wild* means that that species still exists, but that they only live in captivity, such as in a zoo or preservation park. *Critically endangered, endangered,* and *vulnerable* animals are animals that are at risk of extinction in the wild. There are many reasons animals are endangered. Global warming has led to rising water temperatures and the melting of sea ice. Arctic animals are dependent on polar ice platforms to help them hunt, rest, and breed. Water pollution, overfishing, animal poaching, and clearing land for farming and development have also negatively impacted animal habitats.

### BOOKS TO DISPLAY

*Endangered Animals* by Ben Hoare. New York, NY: DK Publishing, 2010.

*Endangered Animals* by Pierre de Hugo. New York, NY: Scholastic, 2007.

*The Tragic Tale of the Great Auk* by Jan Thornhill. Berkeley, CA: Groundwood Books/House of Anansi Press, 2016.

### DID YOU KNOW?

In the North Atlantic, the great auk, a largely flightless bird, once thrived. It was agile in the water and used its small wings as flippers to steer. By 1844, not a single auk could be found. Their demise was partially due to their anatomy, but also because they were hunted for their skins and ornamental eggs. With the auk's extinction, conservationist movements began and laws were passed to prevent the killing of birds during their nesting season. To learn more about the auk, read *The Tragic Tale of the Great Auk* by Jan Thornhill.

# Hands-on Project: Origami Penguin

Penguins are beloved animals, but many species of penguin are threatened with extinction.

## MATERIALS NEEDED

- Square piece of origami paper, preferably one that is black on one side and white on the other side.
- Markers or colored pencils.

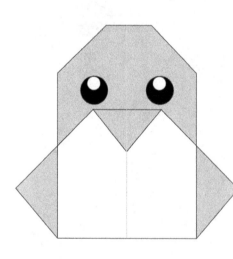

## DIRECTIONS

Give students a square piece of origami paper. If you do not have origami paper, cut a regular piece of paper to make a square. Then have participants follow the directions below and use the diagram shown at right as a guide to create their own origami penguin.

1. Fold the paper in half creating a triangle, crease, then unfold and repeat on the other side.
2. Lay the paper in a diamond shape, with the black side facing up, and fold the bottom corner halfway up toward the center of the diamond.
3. Fold the top edge of the smaller triangle down to create the beak.
4. Turn the paper over.
5. Fold the left and right sides from the top of the diamond halfway to the center to create the penguin's wings.
6. Fold sides along the creases to finish creating the wings.
7. Fold the top of the diamond down toward the center to create the penguin's head.
8. Turn the paper over.
9. Draw on the eyes and decorate your penguin!

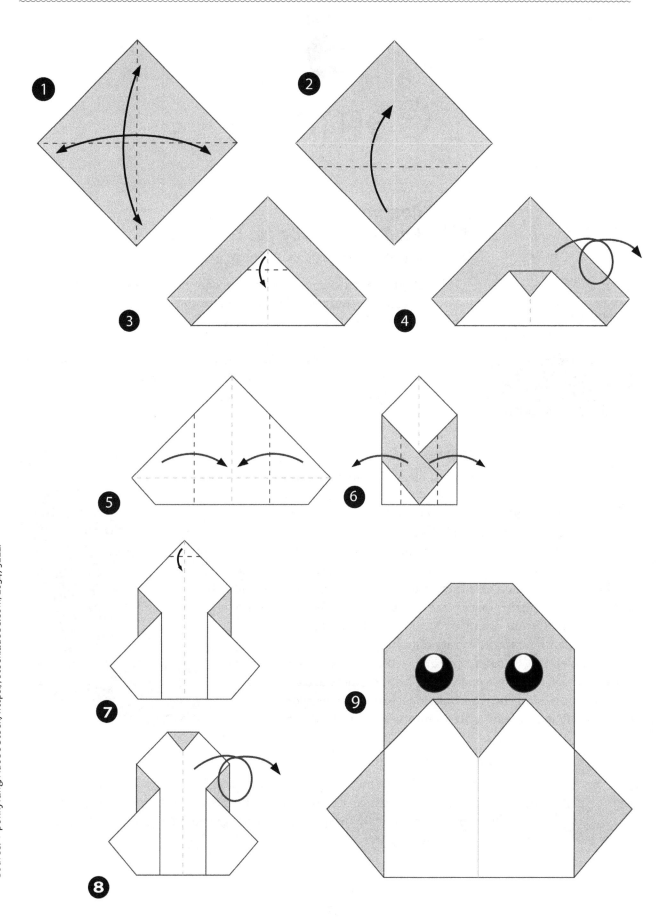

# Compost

### Compost Stew:
### An A to Z Recipe for the Earth

Mary McKenna Siddals. Berkeley, CA: Tricycle Press, 2010.

Rhyming text introduces the concept of composting and the ease of creating compost stew to young readers. This book explains how items break down in the composter and how worms eat their way through the scraps and vegetation, creating a rich black soil that can be used for new plants. The back of the book also provides a list of items not to compost. Collage illustrations created from recycled materials and a variety of papers enhance the text.

### ABOUT COMPOSTING

Composting can be as simple as collecting yard waste and the organic materials from your trash and putting them outside in a pile or bin. Organic trash materials include fruit and vegetable peels, coffee grounds along with the coffee filter, dryer lint, and eggshells. Many people keep a small bin in their kitchen to catch the organic food remains and then take them outside to the larger composting container. Composting takes place as the materials decompose and worms eat the scraps. Compost heaps should contain green items, such as organic scraps and grass clippings, and brown materials, such as fallen leaves, newspaper and wood shavings. Having a mix of items and keeping the compost wet helps promote decomposition. Composting not only benefits individual gardens by providing nutrient rich soil, it also reduces items unnecessarily added to the trash.

### BOOKS TO DISPLAY

*Compost Basics* by Mari Schuh. Mankato, MN: Capstone Press, 2012.

*Save the Planet: Compost It* by David Barker. Ann Arbor, MI: Cherry Lake Publishing, 2010.

*Wiggling Worms at Work* by Wendy Pfeffer. New York, NY: HarperCollins, 2004.

### DID YOU KNOW?

According to the U.S. Environmental Protection Agency, food scraps and yard waste make up about 30 percent of what we throw away. Making compost keeps these items out of landfills where they would take up space and release greenhouse gases, which negatively affect the Earth's atmosphere.

# Hands-on Project

Composting is an easy project for a family, community or school group. Compost bins are simple to make and reinforce reducing waste while instilling recycling habits in children from a young age. Often composting projects are the perfect complement to a garden. Your library likely has many books on both composting and gardening that you can provide to those interested in composting.

## MATERIALS NEEDED

- A container or bin made from whatever you have on hand—old pallets, trash cans, or fencing work well to contain the pile (Alternatively, you can just pick a spot that you will pile your compost.)
- Garden gloves
- Garden shovel
- Compostable materials (yard waste, organic food scraps, etc.)
- Watering can or access to water source
- Cover for the compost container (optional)

## DIRECTIONS

Have participants follow the directions below to start composting at their homes and in their communities.

1. Determine the best location for your compost and place your container in the area.

2. Seek and find compostable waste to add to the compost pile. Try to maintain a 50/50 balance of brown and green items. Greens include produce scraps, grass clippings, coffee grounds, and weeds that have not seeded. Browns include paper towel/toilet paper rolls, newspaper, cardboard, and dried leaves.

3. Add water to your compost to keep it wet like a sponge. Water helps the microbes and insects do their job of breaking down the compost. You can also add a cover to the compost container to keep the compost moist.

4. Stir your compost occasionally to maintain air circulation.

5. Once your compost is ready, you can use it to plant flowers, berries, and vegetables, which thrive in nutrient rich compost.

**LEARN MORE** Purchase or build a worm habitat to see worms in action. Worm habitats are inexpensive and readily available online to purchase. You can also search online for directions on how to build your own habitat for your school or library or share these directions with students or patrons that are interested in building their own. If kids want to see worms, they can easily find worms in compost, garden areas, or under rocks; worms are also more visible after rainfall.

# Gardens and Farms

Phyllis Root    Illustrated by G. Brian Karas

### *Anywhere Farm*

Phyllis Root. Somerville, MA: Candlewick Press, 2017.

Soil, sunshine, water, and a seed—that's what *Anywhere Farm* tells readers they need to start growing plants, flowers, herbs, or vegetables. In this picture book, rhyming text and colorful illustrations encourage young readers to garden, explaining that they can create a farm anywhere—from a boot, to a box, to a backyard. Exploring how a community can come together to create a neighborhood garden, this book shares how anyone can be a farmer.

### ABOUT ANYWHERE GARDENS

You don't need a lot of space to create a garden. Even with a limited amount of space, you can grow flowers, herbs, and vegetables. Simple pots, repurposed containers, and raised beds all make gardening in small spaces possible. Another advantage of small planters is that they can be moved to capture the sun and rain.

### DID YOU KNOW?

Some communities share areas to garden. A community garden is a piece of land that is planted and maintained by a group of people. Community gardens are especially beneficial to those who live in a city and don't have a yard to plant a garden. Cities often have vacant lots that can be turned into community gardens, not only beautifying the area, but also providing valuable gardening space to grow fresh produce. Sharing a community garden also provides the opportunity to interact with your neighbors and create bonds. Read *Farmer Will Allen and the Growing Table* by Jacqueline Briggs Martin to learn more about the urban community garden that was created in Milwaukee, Wisconsin.

### BOOKS TO DISPLAY

*The Curious Garden* by Peter Brown. New York, NY: Little, Brown and Company, 2009.

*Farmer Will Allen and the Growing Table* by Jacqueline Briggs Martin. Bellevue, WA: Readers to Eaters, 2013.

*Up in the Garden and Down in the Dirt* by Kate Messner. San Francisco, CA: Chronicle Books, 2015.

# Hands-on Project

Do you have an old pot, box or bucket that you'd like to repurpose? Find items that can be reused to grow flowers, vegetables, or herbs and repurpose them for this project.

## MATERIALS NEEDED

- Repurposed containers or pots
- Soil
- Seeds or starter plants
- Water
- Acrylic paints and brush or permanent markers

## DIRECTIONS

Have participants follow the instructions below allowing the kids to choose or bring in their own repurposed container or pot. A simple way to add drainage holes is to hammer in and remove a nail in three different locations along the bottom of the container.

1. Choose a gardening pot or other container to repurpose. Try to find one that has holes in the bottom for drainage. If the container chosen does not have holes in the bottom, they will need to be added. Ask an adult for assistance in adding the drainage holes.

2. Using either acrylic paint or permanent markers, decorate the outside of your pot or container as desired. Allow time for paint to dry.

3. Select the flowers or vegetables you want to plant. If starting from seed, carefully read the package about the best time to start them.

4. Determine the best location for your plant making sure it will receive enough sun for it to thrive.

5. Water the plant as needed.

**LEARN MORE**  Food deserts occur in parts of the country that do not have access to fresh fruits, vegetables, or other healthy foods. Food deserts usually happen in impoverished areas where there are many quick-stop food marts that sell processed foods full of sugar and fat, instead of grocery stores or farmers' markets. For more information on food deserts and what is being done to expand the availability of nutritious food, visit **http:// americannutritionassociation.org/newsletter/usda-defines-food-deserts.**

# Farm to Table

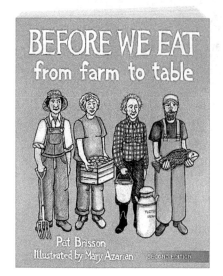

## Before We Eat: From Farm to Table

Pat Brisson. Thomaston, ME: Tilbury House Publishers, 2014.

As a family gathers around a table for a meal, they take time to thank everyone who helped make the food available to them. Farmers, fisherman, truck drivers, and more are recognized, allowing readers to understand all that is involved in preparing food so that we can enjoy a meal. Mary Azarian's illustrations enhance the story, and she produced the images by carving the scenes in wood in reverse, then printing them with ink on paper, and finally enhancing them with acrylic paints.

### ABOUT FARM TO TABLE

Farm to table is a movement that promotes serving local foods at restaurants and school cafeterias. In the past, most of the food found in homes and restaurants was locally sourced. As city populations grew, highways expanded, and refrigerated transportation increased, food was able to be shipped from farther away, and Americans appreciated processed foods and relied on them for time-saving meal preparation. However, in the 1960s and 1970s, people became more health-conscious and wanted access to fresh food. Now it is not uncommon to find farmer's markets open seasonally and many restaurants boast that they serve local foods. Farm to table boosts local economies, supports farmers, and helps the environment. Because products are not shipped long distances, they spend less time on trucks and fewer greenhouse gases are being released into the atmosphere.

### DID YOU KNOW?

The World Resources Institute recently announced that food waste is responsible for eight percent of the annual greenhouse gas emissions. Furthermore, 25

### BOOKS TO DISPLAY

*Farmer Will Allen and the Growing Table* by Jacqueline Briggs Martin. Bellevue, WA: Readers to Eaters, 2013.

*Farming* by Gail Gibbons. New York, NY: Holiday House, 1988.

percent of agricultural water used goes towards producing food that is ultimately uneaten. Food waste is a worldwide issue, but the United States wastes the most—a staggering 40 percent of U.S. food supply each year according to the U.S. Department of Agriculture. Teaching kids the importance of buying only items that they need and keeping food organized at home so they know what they have on hand can help reduce waste. You can teach students about composting and recommend that they consider composting produce that has gone bad instead of throwing it into the trash.

# Hands-on Project

A seed tape is simple to make and will ensure plants are spaced far enough apart so that they grow properly. This is a great activity for kids and adults alike since some seeds are so tiny it makes them difficult to place properly.

## MATERIALS NEEDED

- Toilet paper, single ply or double ply separated
- Elmer's glue
- Several packets of seeds
- Rulers
- Pencils
- Paintbrushes
- Teaspoon
- Magnifying glasses

## DIRECTIONS

Have participants follow the instructions below allowing them to choose which seed they would like to plant. They can bring the paper with the seeds home to plant in their own backyard or if allowed, in your school or library garden!

1. Choose the type of seed you would like to plant.

2. Roll out a length of toilet paper that is manageable to work with. Three to four feet works well.

3. Check the spacing requirements as stated on the seed packet. Using your ruler and pencil, mark the correct spacing for your seeds on the length of toilet paper.

4. Use a paintbrush to apply a dot of Elmer's glue on each of your pencil marks.

5. Place individual seeds on each dot of glue.

6. Allow the pasted seeds to dry.

7. Place the seed tape, seed-side up, in soil at the depth recommended on the seed packet.

**LEARN MORE** Often produce is considered too "ugly" to go to the grocery store. Each year, fruits and vegetables that are not quite perfect account for ten million tons of imperfect food that cannot be sold in stores. This has resulted in the ugly produce movement. Many companies have started selling these imperfect products at a discount. Community shelters and local food banks use the imperfect produce to help combat hunger in communities throughout the world.

# Reimagined Urban Spaces

### *The Curious Garden*

Peter Brown. New York, NY: Little, Brown and Company, 2009.

In this story, young readers discover how neglected, forgotten train tracks can become a lush garden in the city, and enter a magical world where life springs from cracks and crevices. The main character Liam has always wanted to explore the forgotten railway in his city, but when he arrives, he discovers a lonely patch of flowers. Wildflowers and plants are trying to take root, but it is clear they need a gardener. With time, love, and a great deal of learning, Liam's garden thrives and takes over other parts of the abandoned railway and city. Eventually the concrete city is transformed into a lush garden. This wonderful picture book reminds children and adults to look for new ways to beautify and reestablish natural habitats in the world around them.

### ABOUT UNUSED URBAN SPACES AND THE HIGH LINE

One of the best examples of reimagining an unused urban space is the High Line in Manhattan, New York. Originally used as a freight rail line elevated above the streets of Manhattan, the High Line has been transformed into a public park. The first fully functional trains were running on the elevated tracks of the High Line in 1934. By the 1960s, trucks were replacing trains for delivering goods. Eventually sections of the elevated train tracks were demolished, and by 1999, after decades of disuse and neglect, most people were calling for the rest of the High Line to be demolished. However, a thriving garden of wild plants had begun taking over the abandoned structure, giving inspiration to Joshua David and Robert Hammond, who founded the Friends of the High Line, a nonprofit conservancy advocating its preservation and reuse as a public space. In 2009, the first section of the High Line opened to the public. Today the High Line is a 1.45-mile-long greenway, featuring over 500 species of plants and trees. The open public space and gardens also host public events, artwork, and performances. To learn more about the High Line, visit thehighline.org.

### BOOKS TO DISPLAY

*Butterfly Park* by Elly MacKay. Philadelphia, PA: Running Press Kids, 2015.

*Finding Wild* by Megan Wagner Lloyd. New York, NY: Alfred A. Knopf, 2016.

*Florette* by Anna Walker. New York, NY: Clarion Books, 2018.

*On Meadowview Street* by Henry Cole. New York, NY: Greenwillow Books, 2007.

**LEARN MORE** Provide your students with a virtual walking tour of the High Line by visiting **youtube.com/watch?v=jv4m41pbOJE.**

### DID YOU KNOW?

Local parks play a vital role in a city's health. Green spaces keep cities cool and offer a place for recreation. Parks also help people stay healthier and feel better. Around the world, many city planners try to incorporate green spaces, including green roofs, green walls, and pocket parks. Areas that have been abandoned in cities, such as former industrial sites, parking lots, and abandoned infrastructure are being converted into new green spaces. In Seoul, South Korea, the Cheonggyecheon River is viewed as one of the greatest urban design projects. With planning and time, a traffic-choked, elevated freeway and concrete paved polluted waterway has become a 3.6-mile-long planted stream corridor that attracts over 60,000 visitors daily.

# Hands-on Project

Have students reimagine an urban space and create them in shoeboxes.

### MATERIALS NEEDED

- Shoeboxes without lids
- Pom-poms
- Construction paper
- Markers
- Tissue paper
- Glue
- Scissors
- Other assorted items students may want to use and place in their park such as blocks or Legos for benches or small pebbles to create pathways.

### DIRECTIONS

Have participants follow the instructions below and have them think about and then create their reimagined city.

1. Think about a city where you've visited or where you live. Reimagine it with the park you would like to have there. Create your park in a shoebox.

2. Color the inside sides of the shoebox as you imagine your city would look from inside a park area. Does your city have tall buildings? Or maybe mountains in the background?

3. Using the assorted supplies, create a park in the open space of your shoebox. Construction paper can be cut to make picnic tables and other things you may see. Pom-poms can form flowers and trees. Tissue paper can create streams and ponds.

# Seeds

## *The Tree Lady*

H. Joseph Hopkins. New York, NY: Beach Lane Books, 2013.

This picture book follows the true story of Kate Sessions, the first woman to graduate with a degree in science from the University of California, as she starts a movement to add trees and greenery to the once desert town of San Diego, California, and founds Balboa Park. This engaging and motivational book teaches kids to follow their dreams and illustrates the transformation of a city. Today, visitors from all around the world celebrate the beauty and diversity of Balboa Park and its trees.

### ABOUT SEEDS AND BALBOA PARK

In 1868, civic leaders from San Diego, California, set aside 1,400 acres of land for the creation of "City Park." In 1892, Kate Sessions offered to plant 100 trees a year within the park, as well as donate trees and shrubs around San Diego. In exchange, Kate received 32 acres of land within the park for her commercial nursery. When it was announced that San Diego was to host the 1915 Panama-California Exposition, the name City Park was changed to Balboa Park, in honor of Vasco Núñez de Balboa, the first European to spot the Pacific Ocean while on exploration in Panama. Kate thought the park needed more trees for the Exposition, so wrote to gardeners

all over the world asking them to send her seeds that would grow in a desert and traveled to Mexico to look for trees that liked hot, dry weather. Although Balboa Park's current land has been reduced to 1,200 acres, many of Kate's original trees are still alive today. Balboa Park is a wonderful example of how land can be transformed into a beautiful park or garden that everyone can share and enjoy.

### BOOKS TO DISPLAY

*From Seed to Plant* by Gail Gibbons. New York, NY: Holiday House, 1991.

*Miss Maple's Seeds* by Eliza Wheeler. New York, NY: Nancy Paulsen Books, 2013.

*A Seed Is Sleepy* by Dianna Hutts Aston. San Francisco, CA: Chronicle Books, 2007.

*The Tiny Seed* by Eric Carle. Natick, MA: Picture Book Studio, 1987.

### DID YOU KNOW?

Many communities have seed libraries for flowers and vegetables housed in their public libraries and other community buildings. The idea is that patrons can check out a packet of seeds, plant them, allow the plants to mature, and then return seeds to the library when they harvest the next generation of seeds. This exchange allows others to check them out and creates a cycle of seed exchange. If you are interested in starting a seed exchange at your library, you can find a wealth of information on the internet for starting your own or finding one locally.

## Hands-on Project

Share information with participants about native perennial flowers that bloom well in your area and your local state flower, and then help participants plant seeds for these flowers. If you're planning to plant any of these seeds, consider harvesting the seeds the following year to share with a friend or save for a future programming event.

### MATERIALS NEEDED

- Small biodegradable paper cups (non-wax coated) or empty eggshells
- Soil
- Flower or vegetable seeds of your choosing
- Water

### DIRECTIONS

1. Choose which seeds you would like to plant.

2. Place soil in a small paper cup that is not wax coated or in an empty leftover eggshell.

3. Place a seed in the soil.

4. Sprinkle with a small amount of water to moisten the soil.

5. Place the cup in a sunny spot.

6. Check the cup regularly for signs that the seed is sprouting. If the soil seems dry, add a little water.

7. Once the plant is established and the weather is perfect for growing, plant the cup with the plant in the ideal location outside. If you don't have a garden spot to plant, you can use a small pot or repurposed container.

**LEARN MORE** For a short video clip about Kate Sessions, visit this PBS segment at **pbs.org/video/ken-kramers-about-san-diego-kate-sessions-tree-mother-balboa-park**.

# Trees

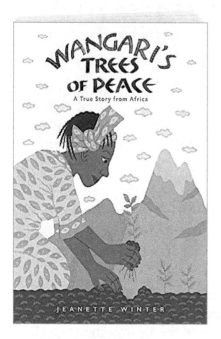

### *Wangari's Trees of Peace: A True Story from Africa*

Jeanette Winter. Orlando, FL: Harcourt, 2008.

This picture book introduces young readers to the story of Wangari Maathai, an environmentalist who was awarded the Nobel Peace Prize in 2004. In the story, Wangari is fearful that clear-cutting the forests of Kenya will result in it becoming barren of its trees and wildlife, so she begins planting seedlings and has women in her village plant small trees in other areas. To encourage the women to help her, she pays each woman a small amount of money if the tree remains alive for at least three months after it's planted. With the help of the local women, she is able to plant over 30 million trees, returning much of Kenya to lush green forests. This inspiring true tale offers kids an introduction to environmental activism.

### ABOUT TREES AND WANGARI MAATHAI

Wangari Maathai was born in Kenya. In 1977, Wangari started the Green Belt Movement in Kenya in response to the deforestation of her homeland, which caused a shortage in firewood, poor soil, erosion, and a shortage in clean drinking water. By 2004, 30 million trees had been planted and 6,000 nurseries existed in Kenya. Trees are essential for life—they release oxygen into the atmosphere, improve air quality, and help filter the water we drink. They also soak up carbon dioxide and other greenhouse gases that cause climate change.

### DID YOU KNOW?

There are many African nations leading the way to fight climate change by planting one tree at a time. The Great Green Wall project was launched by the African Union in 2007 and was funded by the World Bank, the European Union, and the United Nations. The

### BOOKS TO DISPLAY

*Mama Miti: Wangari Maathai and the Trees of Kenya* by Donna Jo Napoli. New York, NY: Simon and Schuster Books for Young Readers, 2010.

*Planting the Trees of Kenya: The Story of Wangari Maathai* by Claire A. Nivola. New York, NY: Farrar, Straus and Giroux, 2008.

*Wangari Maathai: The Woman Who Planted Millions of Trees* by Franck Prévot. Watertown, MA: Charlesbridge, 2015.

goal is to halt the expansion of the Sahara Desert by planting a barrier of trees in Africa's Sahel region. The Great Green Wall plan intends to reforest 247 million acres of land across the width of Africa, from Dakar to Djibouti. The project is due to be complete in 2030, and the restored land is expected to absorb 250 million metric tons of carbon dioxide from the atmosphere.

# Hands-on Project

While plants do not breathe in the sense that humans do, they do respire. Respiration is the process that allows oxygen and carbon dioxide to pass in and out of the plant's stomata, or holes, using diffusion. Using a living plant's leaf, we can observe this happening. This project allows kids to learn about the respiration process.

## MATERIALS NEEDED

- Clear shallow bowl or glass for each student, or allow students to work in pairs
- Water
- A leaf cut from a living flower or plant
- Sunlight

## DIRECTIONS

Have participants follow the instructions below.

1. Fill a shallow bowl with water.

2. Submerge the leaf into the bowl of water. Try to make sure some part of the plant stays underwater for best results.

3. Place the bowl in a sunny location. This will also work in a dark area, but it does take longer. If time allows, place one experiment in a sunny location and another in a dark location. Observe the differences in the bubbles over time.

4. After an hour, check the leaf. Some air bubbles should have formed on the leaf. If time allows, leave the leaf for observation over a longer period of time and watch to see if the bubbles increase or decrease.

### Explaining This Activity

Photosynthesis is the process where plants convert sunlight into chemical energy or food for the plant. As the leaf is taking in carbon dioxide for photosynthesis, it gets rid of the extra oxygen and water it does not need, causing respiration.

**LEARN MORE** Trees are a necessity in humans' lives. They clean the air and protect our drinking water. Many organizations, such as the Arbor Day Foundation, provide free or low-cost native tree seedlings to communities for local restoration projects and schools to distribute to students. Search online or ask at your local nurseries to find a native tree that will thrive in your neighborhood.

# Wildfires

## The Forest of Fire: A Wildfire Story

Erik Ohlsen. Sebastopol, CA: StoryScapes, 2016.

*A Forest of Fire* follows the changes that occur to a pristine forest once humans move into the area. As areas are cleared to provide housing and development, and natural fires are suppressed, disaster strikes with an out-of-control wildfire. After the fire, the magic of the forest begins as plants and trees rejuvenate, allowing people to learn that controlled burns help the forest stay healthy. Rhyming text explains how people affect the natural cycle of forests and encourages us to work with nature.

### ABOUT WILDFIRES

Wildfires are a natural part of the life cycle in the wilderness. Some evergreen trees are dependent on fire to release their seeds, while other trees and shrubs grow back quickly after a fire providing food for animals on the forest floor. Many insects also thrive and lay their eggs in post-fire conditions. Naturally occurring wildfires often renew the forests. They eliminate "fuel" that can accumulate on the forest floor, such as leaves, dead wood, twigs and bark. Wildfires also thin out old, dying trees and other plants, allowing more sunlight to reach the forest floor. Fires need three things to burn; fuel, oxygen and heat, and are caused by a burning match, a flash of lightning, or a glowing ember. Ground fires are slow-moving fires that burn dead, rotting leaves and roots of plants on the ground. Surface fires move along the forest floor from plant to plant burning fallen leaves and branches. Crown fires are extremely dangerous and spread in the tops of trees. Winds cause crown fires to quickly change direction. Droughts make wildfires more frequent and extreme. A warming climate can cause shorter winters and long, hot summers. With drought conditions, not enough precipitation occurs causing forests to dry out, allowing wildfires to quickly grow out of control endangering animals and communities.

### BOOKS TO DISPLAY

*Little Lost Tiger* by Jonathan London. Tarrytown, NY: Marshall Cavendish Children, 2012.

*Wildfires* by Kathy Furgang. Washington, DC: National Geographic, 2015.

*Wildfires* by Seymour Simon. New York, NY: HarperCollins Publishers, 2016.

### DID YOU KNOW?

The Amazon Rainforest experienced a dramatic increase of fires. Between January and August 2019, Brazil's National Institute for Space Research showed almost 46,000 active fire hot spots within the Amazon. Unlike fires in other parts of the world, these are not a natural part of the rainforest. Deforestation caused by human activity has broken the typical rainforest moisture cycle, meaning less moisture is making it into the atmosphere and is drying out the rainforest, which allows for the spread of fires. The typical moisture cycle in rainforests provides sufficient rain for farmers and for the rainforests to maintain enough moisture in the air to sustain a healthy ecosystem. When the typical moisture cycle is broken, it can lead to droughts and forest fires, like it has in the Amazon Rainforest.

## Hands-on Project

Fires require three things to burn—heat, oxygen, and fuel. These components are known as the fire triangle. Firefighters know that if you eliminate one element from the fire triangle, the fire will go out. Create your own fire triangle and describe what you could do to put out the fire and what fire element was removed.

### MATERIALS NEEDED

- Construction paper
- Pencil
- Crayons or markers

### DIRECTIONS

Have participants follow the instructions below.

1. Draw someone putting out or preventing a fire.

2. Discuss how the fire is being controlled. What element is being eliminated from the fire triangle?

3. Color the picture and share with the class.

**LEARN MORE** The lodgepole pine tree has two kinds of pinecones. One opens naturally over time and its winged seeds whirl to the forest floor. The other type of seed is sealed in a rock-hard pine resin that only opens when the heat of a fire burns away the resin. Naturally occurring wildfires are essential for releasing these seeds. Pinecones are hygroscopic, meaning they soak up water. Pinecone seeds are located on each scale. If a pinecone has absorbed too much water, the scales swell and close. When the cone is warm and dry, the scales open, releasing the seeds in the wind. Take a nature walk with your students and have them collect a few pinecones. Place them in water to see the scales close. After the pinecone is closed, take it out of the water, and place it in a dry, sunny location to see them reopen.

# Coral Reefs

## The Brilliant Deep: Rebuilding the World's Coral Reefs: The Story of Ken Nedimyer and the Coral Restoration Foundation

Kate Messner. San Francisco, CA: Chronicle Books, 2018.

Perfect for young readers, this book shares the true story of Ken Nedimyer, an environmental scientist who loves the ocean and the brilliantly colored coral reefs off the Florida coast. Using a hammer, glue, and living rocks, Ken decides to save the coral. The story of Ken's progress in restoring the coral reefs, as well as the creation of the Coral Restoration Foundation, is told in an assessable picture book format. The story is enhanced with beautiful illustrations and more details on coral reefs can be found at the end of the book.

### ABOUT CORAL REEFS

Coral reefs are built by tiny sea animals called coral polyps, each the size of a grain of rice. Polyps attach themselves to the skeletons of dead coral and add layers to form new coral reefs. There are two types of coral animals—hard coral and soft coral polyps. Hard coral colonies have a similar appearance as pillars, cacti, horns, and even brains. Soft coral colonies look like fans, fingers, flowers, or multicolored swaying feathers. A variety of fish and sea creatures make their home in coral reefs, including sea anemone, urchins, and clown fish. Coral reefs are home to 25 percent of all marine fish species. Unfortunately, coral reefs are dying at an alarming rate. Today, there is half as much coral in the Caribbean as there was in the 1970s. Scientists believe that changing ocean temperatures, disease, boating, and overfishing have contributed to the problem.

> **BOOKS TO DISPLAY**
>
> *Extreme Coral Reef! Q & A* by Melissa Stewart. Washington, DC: Smithsonian, 2008.
>
> *Life in a Coral Reef* by Wendy Pfeffer. New York, NY: HarperCollins, 2009.
>
> *Over in the Ocean: In a Coral Reef* by Marianne Berkes. Nevada City, CA: Dawn Pu

### DID YOU KNOW?

Coral bleaching is a term used when corals lose their algae due to a stress response, causing them to turn pale or completely white. Coral bleaching is caused by a range of environmental issues such as pollution, oil spills, extreme sea temperatures, and disease. Bleached corals are still living and can survive the bleaching event if environmental conditions improve quickly. However, prolonged environmental events can lead to the death of the corals, and bleached corals are more susceptible to disease and death.

# Hands-on Project

Coral reefs are colorful and thriving with life. Create a mural of a coral reef with your class, or have children work on their own individual projects. Use the internet or magazines to reference images of a coral reef.

## MATERIALS NEEDED

- Mural-size piece of blue paper or individual paper
- Washable paints, markers, and crayons

## DIRECTIONS

Share pictures of coral reefs and animals with participants and provide them information about the different types of coral there are. Decide if participants will be working alone or on a large mural for the room. If working on a mural, assign children a specific section. Once you have decided whether participants will be working on a large mural or working alone, have them follow the instructions below:

1. After studying pictures of the reef and animals, create your own colorful coral reef.

2. Think about what types of coral you'd like to create and what colors to use. If working on a mural, make sure to work on your assigned section.

3. Draw the sea animals that live on or around the reef.

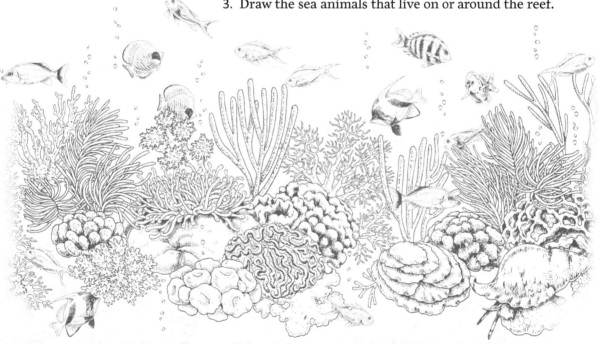

Source: val_iva / Adobe Stock

**LEARN MORE** Comprised of nearly 3,000 separate reefs and more than 900 tropical islands, the Great Barrier Reef in Australia stretches over 1,400 miles. The Great Barrier Reef contains 400 types of coral, 1,500 species of fish, and 4,000 types of mollusk. The Great Barrier Reef is one of the Seven Natural Wonders of the World. The Great Barrier Reef Marine Park website provides information and a short introduction video on the reef, which is available at **gbrmpa.gov.au/**.

# Estuaries

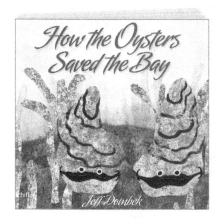

## How the Oysters Saved the Bay

Jeff Dombek. Atglen, PA: Schiffer Publishing Ltd, 2013.

This environment tale teaches young children about how oysters filter and clean seawater and follows oysters Chester and Meredith as they realize that pollution in the Chesapeake Bay is affecting the health of the underwater grasses. The only way that the underwater grasses can get enough sunlight to grow is if the water is clear. The oysters know they have the ability to clear up the murky, polluted water, and they set off to improve the water and the grasses, which provide a much needed habitat for all the animals in the bay.

### ABOUT ESTUARIES

Estuaries are found where freshwater and saltwater meet. For example, they can be found at the edge of oceans, where rivers and streams run into the sea. The area where the water mixes is called brackish water. The amount of salt in an estuary changes as water moves in and out. Estuaries are important for filtering water and protecting the shore from storm waves. They are essential to the ecosystem and provide habitats for many animals. Salt marshes and mangrove forests can also be found within estuaries.

### DID YOU KNOW?

Oysters are made to live in estuaries. When the tide goes out, oysters close their shells, and they reopen them when the tide comes in. Oysters pull algae and plankton from the water and are a keystone species that are essential for maintaining a healthy coastal ecosystem. Oysters also act as effective shoreline buffers and oyster reefs provide a habitat for numerous species. Oysters have been negatively affected by many factors including climate change, over harvesting, and water pollution. Many organizations, such as the Chesapeake Bay Foundation, have begun oyster reef restoration

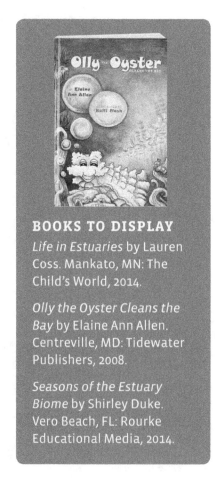

### BOOKS TO DISPLAY

*Life in Estuaries* by Lauren Coss. Mankato, MN: The Child's World, 2014.

*Olly the Oyster Cleans the Bay* by Elaine Ann Allen. Centreville, MD: Tidewater Publishers, 2008.

*Seasons of the Estuary Biome* by Shirley Duke. Vero Beach, FL: Rourke Educational Media, 2014.

projects to rejuvenate the declining oyster population and repair the ecosystem. Used oyster and clam shells from local watermen and restaurants are collected and disinfected by volunteers to be used when creating new oyster reefs. New oysters attach to the shells of old oysters, naturally growing the reefs and repopulating the estuaries.

# Hands-on Project

When salt is in water, it adds mass to the water, making water denser than it would normally be. This density allows objects and people to float better in saltwater than in freshwater, as is seen when you float in the ocean. Have kids try floating objects in both freshwater and saltwater to see if they will sink or float.

## MATERIALS NEEDED

- Three containers all the same shape and size per child
- Water
- Table salt
- Teaspoon
- A variety of small items, such as a cork, paper clip, penny, ball of foil, etc.

## DIRECTIONS

Have participants follow the instructions below to determine which items sink or float in fresh and saltwater.

1. Fill each container with equal amounts of water, about 1 cup.

2. Leave one container with plain freshwater.

3. Add 1 teaspoon of salt to the second container.

4. Add 2 teaspoons of salt to the third container.

5. With each object, predict whether the item will sink or float in each of your containers, then test to see if your prediction is correct. Always start with the freshwater, so you don't accidentally contaminate that container with salt after testing the objects.

6. If you want to add more salt to additional containers, test heavier objects to see at which point they will float.

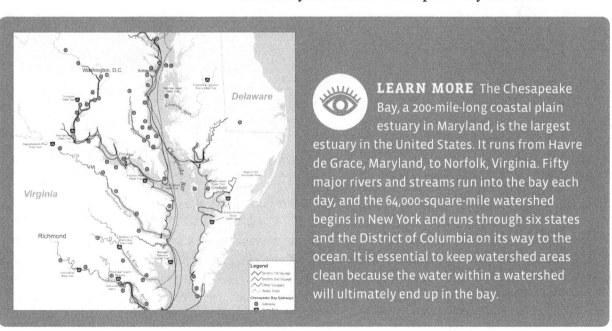

**LEARN MORE** The Chesapeake Bay, a 200-mile-long coastal plain estuary in Maryland, is the largest estuary in the United States. It runs from Havre de Grace, Maryland, to Norfolk, Virginia. Fifty major rivers and streams run into the bay each day, and the 64,000-square-mile watershed begins in New York and runs through six states and the District of Columbia on its way to the ocean. It is essential to keep watershed areas clean because the water within a watershed will ultimately end up in the bay.

# Galápagos Islands

## *Galápagos Girl/Galapagueña*

Marsha Diane Arnold. New York, NY: Lee & Low Books, 2018.

This bilingual book explores the fictional life of Valentina Cruz, who grew up on her family's farm on the Galápagos Island of Floreana. While the original tortoises on Floreana are extinct, Valentina grows up with tortoises that had been brought to the island from other neighboring islands. Her love for all the Galápagos animals inspires her to become a biologist as an adult. During Valentina's career, she works to protect the many animals in threat of extinction.

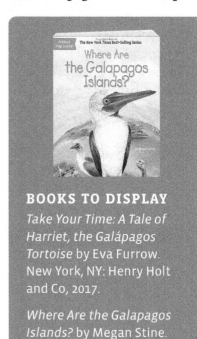

### ABOUT THE GALÁPAGOS ISLANDS

The Galápagos Islands are located in the Pacific Ocean, about 600 miles off the coast of Ecuador in South America. They consist of 13 major islands and more than 100 small islands and rocks formed by volcanoes. Many of the plants and animals found in the Galápagos are endemic, meaning that they are not found anywhere else on earth. These include the Galápagos tortoise, the Galápagos marine iguana, the Galápagos blue butterfly, and the Floreana mockingbird. The growing population, tourist trade, and changing climate have greatly affected the islands. Invasive species such as goats, rats, and pigs have negatively impacted these distinct natives, making them more at risk of becoming extinct.

### BOOKS TO DISPLAY

*Take Your Time: A Tale of Harriet, the Galápagos Tortoise* by Eva Furrow. New York, NY: Henry Holt and Co, 2017.

*Where Are the Galapagos Islands?* by Megan Stine. New York, NY: Grosset and Dunlap, 2017.

### DID YOU KNOW?

The Galápagos tortoise has an average lifespan of 100 years or more. They typically reach a weight of 475 pounds and can grow to be about 4 feet long. Saddle-backed tortoises inhabit the hotter, drier islands that have sparse vegetation. Unlike domed tortoises, saddle-backed tortoises have long necks, long legs, and a shell shape that lets them extend their heads up high to reach bushes and trees. Domed tortoises live on wetter islands that have vegetation close to the ground. They are better protected against attacks from predators because they can draw their neck and head into their dome shells.

Source: Maridav / Adobe Stock

# Hands-on Project

The average Galápagos tortoise is 4 feet long. Using brown butcher paper and a measuring tape, have the children compare their height to the length of the tortoise.

## MATERIALS NEEDED

- Roll of brown butcher paper
- Pencil
- Measuring tape
- Colored pencils, markers, stickers

## DIRECTIONS

1. Roll out a long sheet of brown butcher paper and have the child lay down on the paper with their feet near the bottom of the paper.

2. Using a pencil, create an outline of the child.

3. Indicate the height of the child by measuring from the top of their head to the heel of their feet on the paper and note the size comparison to that of a Galápagos tortoise. Is the child's length greater or less than that of the tortoise?

4. Using crayons or markers, have the child create and decorate a "shell" pattern within their outline.

**LEARN MORE** To learn more about the Galápagos Tortoise, read *Take Your Time: A Tale of Harriet, the Galápagos Tortoise* by Eva Furrow at an upcoming storytime. Harriet the tortoise does everything slowly, too slowly according to the other island animals who feel she is missing out on life. Harriet explores the wildlife and islands of the Galápagos, but discovers that while the world around her is wonderful, she still loves her home best. Have your students or patrons discover the size and grandeur of the Galápagos Tortoise with this video from BBC: **youtube.com/watch?v=rEp6pkkYOgE.**

# Garbage and Recycling

### *Recycle! A Handbook for Kids*

Gail Gibbons. Boston, MA: Little, Brown and Company, 1992.

Gail Gibbons is known for her thorough and approachable explanations of real-world topics for children. *Recycle!* explains the process of recycling for each type of material, including how long these products take to break down in the landfill if we choose not to recycle them. The book provides practical tips to help you and your students start reducing waste in the world.

### ABOUT RECYCLING

Beginning in the twentieth century, people began to throw out much more waste. As items were less expensive to manufacture and purchase, we became a more disposable society where things were bought and thrown away instead of being repaired or reused. Items also began being wrapped and shipped in plastic materials, much of which cannot be recycled. Over 90 percent of all plastic created has not been recycled. About 20,000 plastic bottles are purchased each second; yet, less than half of these bottles are recycled. There are several methods of collecting recyclable goods. Some areas have receptacles for each type of material, while others have single-stream recycling, where all items are mixed within one container and sorted at a recycling center. Plastic never decomposes; instead, it breaks down into smaller pieces of plastic called microplastics. Not only can animals become entangled in pieces of plastic, they can often mistake it for food and consume it. Microplastics have also been found in our food, including table salt and tap water. Cardboard, paper, and some hard plastics, such as milk jugs and laundry soap containers can be easily recycled.

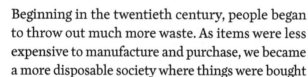

### BOOKS TO DISPLAY

*Fly Guy Presents: Garbage and Recycling* by Ted Arnold. New York, NY: Scholastic, 2019.

*Michael Recycle* by Ellie Bethel. San Diego, CA: IDW Publications, 2012.

*Trash Revolution: Breaking the Waste Cycle* by Erica Fyvie. Toronto, ON: Kids Can Press, Ltd: 2018.

*What a Waste: Trash* by Jess French. New York, NY: DK Publishing, 2019.

*What a Waste: Where Does Garbage Go?* by Claire Eamer. Berkeley: Annick Press Ltd., 2017.

**DID YOU KNOW?**
Massive trash piles are known as landfill sites. As waste decomposes, greenhouse gasses, such as methane and carbon dioxide, are produced. Rain and storm water runoff moving through the landfill can collect toxic particles and poison nearby groundwater. This can pose a serious health risk as more people are living closer to landfill sites. Individuals can help by volunteering to clean up and properly dispose of trash, making sure recyclable items are disposed of properly, and urging businesses to reduce their waste.

# Hands-on Project

Having containers in multiple locations in your home and classroom will help you and your students recycle appropriate items instead of throwing them in the trash.

## MATERIALS NEEDED

- Repurposed cardboard boxes
- Markers
- Crayons
- Stickers
- Other decorations as desired

## DIRECTIONS

Have participants follow the instructions below to make recycling containers.

1. Using a repurposed cardboard box, decorate the container as desired. Think about if your container will be for all recyclable items, or if you will need different containers for the different items.

2. Think about an area where you often have items that need to be recycled. Maybe a bedroom, family room, or office at home? Or if there's a large classroom, having containers in different workspaces could be helpful. And place your container in the area where you most often find items that need to be recycled.

**LEARN MORE** Much of our trash ends up in our oceans and other waterways. The city of Baltimore, Maryland, has a unique solution to remove waste from their harbor—Mr. Trash Wheel, a semi-autonomous trash interceptor that is placed at the end of a river, stream, or other waterway. In 2014, Mr. Trash Wheel was the first of four such wheels installed in the area and was placed at the Jones Falls Stream, where it enters the Inner Harbor. Mr. Trash Wheel is powered by the sun and the current of the river. It has a giant 14-foot water wheel that pulls trash onto its conveyor belt and drops it into a dumpster sitting on a separate floating barge. Since its inception, Mr. Trash wheel has collected more than 1,000,000 pounds of trash. To find out more about Mr. Trash Wheel and see a video of him in action, visit **mrtrashwheel.com**.

# Plastic Bags

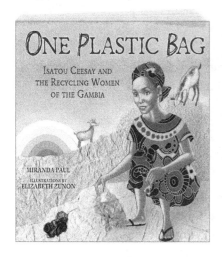

## *One Plastic Bag: Isatou Ceesay and the Recycling Women of the Gambia*

Miranda Paul. Minneapolis: Millbrook Press, 2015.

In this true story, Isatou Ceesay, a village woman, notices that there are plastic bags littering her home in Gambia. As the bags accumulate, goats begin to die from eating the plastic and gardens struggle to grow in the trash filled soil. Isatou decides to try to solve the problem, and with the help of other village women, begins making purses from the plastic bags. At first, the villagers laugh at the women, but as the purses start to become a success, they eventually see the benefit to the community. This book shows how one person can make a difference and inspire change.

### ABOUT PLASTIC BAGS

Lightweight single-use plastic bags are a threat to the environment. They can travel long distances over land and often end up in streams, rivers, and oceans. They do not biodegrade in waterways; instead, they break into smaller pieces that are consumed by animals. Up to 80 percent of plastic found in the ocean enters from the land. It is believed that up to 267 different species have been affected by plastic pollution in the ocean, and every year an estimated 100,000 marine animals are killed by plastic bags. The average American family takes home almost 1,500 plastic shopping bags per year; yet, only one percent is returned for recycling. Reusable shopping bags are an easy way to eliminate this threat to our environment.

### DID YOU KNOW?

In the United States, California became the first and only state as of yet to ban single-use plastic bags in 2014. Retailers must use either a reusable eco-friendly bag or recyclable paper bag. In a 2019 United Nations Environment report, at least 127 countries had legislation to regulate single-use plastic.

### BOOKS TO DISPLAY

*The Adventures of a Plastic Bottle* by Alison Inches. New York, NY: Little Simon, 2009.

*Tracking Trash: Flotsam, Jetsam, and the Science of Ocean Motion* by Loree Griffin Burns. Boston: Houghton Mifflin, 2007.

# Hands-on Project

"Plarn" is yarn made from plastic bags, which are abundant. Turning plastic bags into a usable product is a great way to reduce waste and reuse an item. Plarn can be used to crochet and to make tote bags and purses. In this project, participants will learn how to create a jump rope from plarn.

## MATERIALS NEEDED

- 12 plastic bags per participant
- Scissors
- Duct tape
- Painter's tape

## DIRECTIONS

Have participants follow the instructions below to create plarn and make a jump rope.

1. Cut off the handles and bottoms of 12 bags.

2. Cut the bag sides at their seams. This will form two large rectangles from each bag.

3. Cut each rectangle into long strips.

4. Tie 12 strips together to form the length of the rope. Add more strips if needed for additional length. Repeat for a total of six lengths of rope.

5. At one end, use duct tape to secure six lengths of rope together, creating a handle.

6. Use painter's tape to secure the handle to a surface.

7. Braid all six lengths of rope together and secure the end with duct tape to create a second handle.

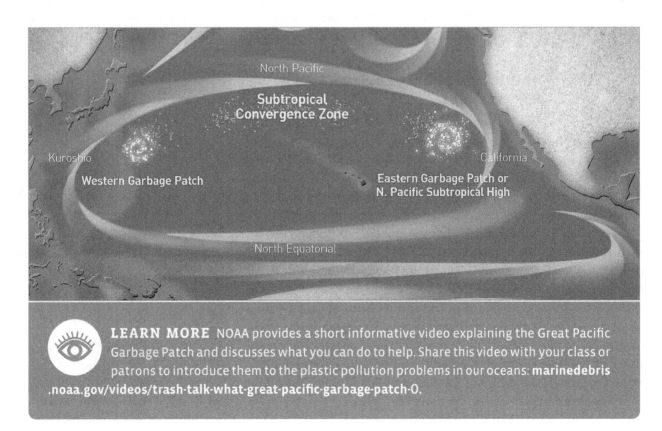

**LEARN MORE** NOAA provides a short informative video explaining the Great Pacific Garbage Patch and discusses what you can do to help. Share this video with your class or patrons to introduce them to the plastic pollution problems in our oceans: **marinedebris .noaa.gov/videos/trash-talk-what-great-pacific-garbage-patch-0**.

# Recycled Instruments

## *Ada's Violin: The Story of the Recycled Orchestra of Paraguay*

Susan Hood. New York, NY: Simon and Schuster Books for Young Readers, 2016.

Based on a true story, this picture book follows Ada, who is from the town of Cateura, Paraguay. One of the poorest towns in South America, Cateura serves as the main garbage dump for the capital city of Paraguay. People from Cateura typically live on less than two dollars a day. The main job for families from there is to pick through the trash in the landfill and look for items they can recycle or sell. While Ada dreams of music, she must deal with the realities of living in this town. When children in the neighborhood are offered music lessons, they quickly discover there are not enough instruments for all who want to play. Eventually, many people from the town come together to create instruments from trash and an orchestra blooms. This true story reminds readers young and old that ingenuity and hard work can solve problems and create solutions even amid despair.

### ABOUT THE RECYCLED ORCHESTRA OF PARAGUAY

The recycled orchestra was founded by Favio Chavez, an environmental engineer working in Cateura, a landfill near Asunción, Paraguay, that receives about three million pounds of waste every day. Chavez noticed that the children either ended up working in the landfill or joining gangs, so he decided to teach interested children music in his free time. Soon he realized that there were not enough instruments, and even if there were instruments, they were at risk of being stolen because they were worth more than a home in Cateura. Chavez asked a talented local carpenter if he could make instruments for the children from things found in the landfill. Drumheads have been made from old X-ray film, and saxophones have been made out of drainpipes, coins, bottle caps, and more. The orchestra has gained notoriety and has even performed for politicians, monarchs, and Pope Francis. They have also performed with famous musicians including Stevie Wonder and the band Metallica.

### BOOKS TO DISPLAY

*One Plastic Bag: Isatou Ceesay and the Recycling Women of the Gambia* by Miranda Paul. Minneapolis, MN: Millbrook Press, 2015.

*A Plastic Bottle's Journey* by Suzanne Slade. Mankato, MN: Picture Window Books, 2011.

*Trash Revolution: Breaking the Waste Cycle* by Erica Fyvie. Toronto, Ontario: Kids Can Press, 2018.

**DID YOU KNOW?**

The United States generates a lot of trash each year, approximately 230 million tons! How much is a ton? The average female African elephant weighs three tons! Each person in the United States creates about four and a half pounds of trash daily, with less than one quarter being recycled. To have your students understand how much waste they produce, have them carry a bag with them for the school day and collect all the trash that they produce in that bag. Recyclable and compostable items can be disposed of properly, but any items that would normally be placed in the trash should be placed in the bag they carry throughout the day. At the end of the day, pile the bags together to see just how much trash your class has accumulated. After doing this activity, discuss how much waste each student ended their day with. Ask students if it was more or less than they expected and if there are ways they can recycle and compost more items. You can also recommend this activity for students to do at home, so they can compare results with other family members.

# Hands-on Project

Using a variety of recycled objects, have kids create their own musical instruments. After the instruments are complete, have the students perform a concert at the end of class.

## MATERIALS NEEDED

- Recycled and clean cardboard boxes and shoeboxes
- Recycled and clean cardboard containers, paper towel tubes, and toilet paper tubes
- Plastic bottles with caps
- Plastic containers with lids
- Old CDs
- Plastic straws
- Scissors
- Duct tape
- Rubber bands
- String and ribbon
- Dried beans and other filling materials
- Disposable chopsticks
- Crayons, Sharpie markers, and other items to decorate the instruments

## DIRECTIONS

Have participants follow the instructions below to create an instrument of their choice.

1. Use a variety of recycled and household materials to create your own musical instruments. Drums can be made easily from containers with lids, and disposable chopsticks make perfect drumsticks. Guitars can be crafted from shoeboxes and rubber bands. Rain sticks and maracas are easy percussion instruments to make. Plastic straws can be cut in various lengths and taped from shortest to longest to make a pan flute. The ideas are endless; let your imagination guide you.

2. After crafting your instrument, decorate and enjoy!

**LEARN MORE** Have your students watch this video to hear the Recycled Orchestra of Paraguay play: **youtube.com/watch?v=5sOHfxdes1A**.

# Renewable Energy

## *The Boy Who Harnessed the Wind* Picture Book Edition

William Kamkwamba and Bryan Mealer. New York, NY: Dial Books for Young Readers, 2012.

This inspiring true story follows a young boy, William, and his family, as his village in Malawi suffers through a drought. William turns to books to look for a solution to combat the drought. In his village library, he learns about windmills and has the idea to build one to help his family. Using scrap metal and old parts found around the village, William brings electricity to his home, allowing his family to pump the water they need to farm their land. This story reminds us that one person can make a difference, regardless of their age, and often books provide the answers we are seeking.

### ABOUT RENEWABLE ENERGY

Renewable energy comes from resources that will never run out. Wind, rivers, and sunlight are examples of renewable resources. Nonrenewable resources, such as coal, oil, and natural gas, emit carbon dioxide. Carbon dioxide is a gas produced as waste when fossil fuels are burned for energy. When we produce large amounts of carbon dioxide, heat is trapped inside the Earth's atmosphere. This is called the greenhouse effect. Global warming happens when the average temperature of the Earth increases over time. This warming can have consequences for all living things. Summers become hotter, winters become colder, and storms become fiercer. Many scientists also believe global warming is causing the ice caps at the North and South poles to melt. Melting ice caps change the water levels in the ocean and affect animals like polar bears and penguins (see chapter 6 for more information on melting ice caps and polar bears).

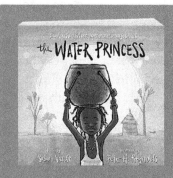

### BOOKS TO DISPLAY

*Energy Island: How One Community Harnessed the Wind and Changed Their World* by Allan Drummond. New York, NY: Farrar, Straus and Giroux, 2011.

*The Water Princess* by Susan Verde. New York, NY: G.P. Putnam's Sons, 2016.

*What Does It Mean to Go Green?* by Molly Aloian. St. Catherines, Ontario: Crabtree Publishing Co., 2014.

### DID YOU KNOW?

Windmills were invented over a 1,000 years ago in the Middle East, in the area now known as Iran, and were used to grind corn and pump water. The modern wind turbine now makes electric power. When wind blows across a turbine's blade, the blade turns and causes the main shaft to spin a generator, creating electric power. The electricity generated by wind turbines can be used to power a single home or building, or it can be connected to an energy grid where the whole community shares the electricity.

# Hands-on Project

Windmills have been used for years to harness the wind and create energy. Have participants make their own basic pinwheel to demonstrate the wind's power.

### MATERIALS NEEDED

- 5″ x 5″ square of card stock or other sturdy paper
- Rulers
- Scissors
- Pencils
- Glue
- Straws
- Thumbtacks

### DIRECTIONS

Have participants follow the instructions below to create their own pinwheels.

1. Cut a 5″ x 5″ piece of card stock. If you do not have card stock, glue two sheets of paper together to achieve a thicker, sturdier paper.

2. Using your ruler, draw a diagonal line from one corner of the paper to the other. Repeat drawing a line between the remaining two corners, creating an X on the paper.

3. Make a 2″ cut along each line from the corner toward the center.

4. Fold the corners of the square toward the center, one at a time, gluing each corner to the other. You may have to hold the corners together in the center until the glue sets.

5. When the glue is dry, position a plastic straw along the back of the pinwheel. Place a thumbtack in the center of the pinwheel to secure it to the straw. Be sure the thumbtack does not poke out past the back of the straw. If you do not have a straw, you can also attach the pinwheel to a paper towel tube, pencil eraser, or paper cup.

6. Set it in the wind and watch the pinwheel spin.

**LEARN MORE** The sun is one of Earth's many sources of renewable energy. Solar panels capture the sun's energy and generate a flow of electricity. There are simple ways to harness the sun's energy, including making a solar oven, which can slow cook food. Numerous sources can be found on the internet for making a solar oven with simple instructions and easy recipes. For a fun experiment, have your students try making a treat in an outdoor solar oven. Just remember it will take a much longer amount of time to cook.

# Water Conservation

## *Splash! Water*

Nuria Jiménez and Empar Jiménez. Hauppauge, NY: Barron's, 2010.

One of Earth's most precious resources is water. This book explains the importance that water plays in people's lives as well the scarcity of clean water worldwide in ways children can relate to. For example, did you know that if a pitcher held all the water on Earth and you poured it into 100 glasses, only one glass would hold drinkable freshwater? Filled with practical suggestions for what people can do to conserve water, this picture book covers everything that kids need to know about water conservation in ways they can understand. Colorful pictures enhance the text and activities are included at the end of the book to reinforce the topic of water conservation.

### ABOUT WATER CONSERVATION

Seventy percent of the Earth's surface is covered with water! However, 97.5 percent of water on Earth is saltwater, which is not drinkable. Freshwater makes up only 2.5 percent of the Earth's water, but much of that is frozen in polar ice caps and glaciers. That means only about one percent of all the water on Earth is available for human use. The U.S. Environmental Protection Agency anticipates at least 40 states will have water shortages by 2024. Many areas of the United States are experiencing an increased frequency, duration, and intensity of droughts, making water conservation essential. Climate change has caused droughts in some places and flooding in others. Droughts leave rivers and lakes dry, while flash floods cause dirt and runoff to fill our water supply, making fresh water undrinkable. The practice of using water efficiently to reduce unnecessary water waste and usage benefits everyone on Earth. Worldwide, billions of people do not have access to safe drinking water. Often women and girls in rural areas in countries such as Kenya, India, and Bolivia are responsible for walking miles each day to the closest water source to collect water, making it impossible for them to go to school or work.

### BOOKS TO DISPLAY

*Clean Water* by Ellen Labrecque. Ann Arbor, MI: Cherry Lake Publishing, 2018.

*Save Water* by Kay Barnham. New York, NY: Crabtree Publishing Co., 2008.

*The Water Princess* by Susan Verde. New York, NY: G.P. Putnam's Sons, 2016.

### DID YOU KNOW?

Xeriscaping is a landscaping practice that uses many native, drought-resistant plants arranged in an efficient, water-saving layout. Grouping plants according to their watering needs, maximizing shady areas for planting, eliminating traditional lawn grass, and using mulch contribute to a landscape that conserves water.

# Hands-on Project

The water cycle is the process where water circulates between the Earth's bodies of water, atmosphere, and land. Precipitation happens in the form of rain or snow and then drains into streams and rivers, returning to the atmosphere by evaporation. With this project, your students can witness the water cycle.

### MATERIALS NEEDED

- Clear recycled plastic bottles with caps or other sealed plastic containers
- Water
- Sunny spot

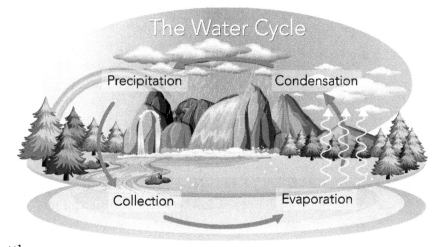

### DIRECTIONS

Have participants follow the instructions below to learn about the water cycle.

1. Pour water into a plastic bottle.

2. Place the cap on the bottle or seal it, so that the water and air cannot escape.

3. Place the closed bottle in a sunny spot.

4. Be patient. Take notice of the changes during the day. With time you will see condensation collect on the sides of the bottle and it will start "raining" from the top. Take your bottle home to place in a sunny location to continue to observe the differences that occur when it is sunny, cloudy, warm, or cold.

**LEARN MORE** The average U.S. citizen uses 50–80 gallons of water per day, more than any other country. In Africa, by comparison, the average family uses just five gallons per day. The official website for U.S. Homeland Security has tips for many emergency situations, including water conservation and drought readiness. To learn more about ways you and your students can be prepared, **visit ready.gov/drought**.

# Hurricanes

### A Penguin Named Patience:
### A Hurricane Katrina Rescue Story

Suzanne Lewis. Ann Arbor, MI: Sleeping Bear Press, 2015.

In August 2005, Hurricane Katrina makes landfall in New Orleans, causing monumental damage to the area. While the Audubon Aquarium of the Americas initially survives the hurricane, repeated electrical outages and damage to the aquarium makes it impossible to keep the animals there. Nineteen penguins, including Patience, are temporarily transported to Monterey Aquarium in California while the Audubon Aquarium is being repaired. *A Penguin Named Patience* tells the story of this amazing rescue and the cooperation among the aquariums in saving the penguins. The book serves as a wonderful reminder that even in difficult times, coming together as a community can help us find solutions.

### ABOUT HURRICANES

Hurricanes, or tropical cyclones, begin as thunderstorms over warm tropical ocean waters near the equator. Warm, moist air from the ocean's surface begins to rise rapidly where it encounters cooler air. As the storm moves over the ocean, it grows larger, its wind speed increases, and it begins to rotate. A tropical cyclone that has a maximum sustained surface wind of less than 38 mph is considered a tropical depression. Tropical storms have a maximum sustained surface wind of 39–74mph. Hurricanes have a maximum sustained surface winds of 74 mph or greater. Due to the Earth's rotation, hurricanes that form in the northern part of the world spin counterclockwise, while those that form in the south spin clockwise. Hurricanes are categorized by their continuous wind speed on the Saffir-Simpson Hurricane Wind Scale. The scale estimates potential property damage, with those rated a Category 3 or higher considered major hurricanes because of their potential for loss of life and damage. Most hurricanes that affect the Americas form off the west coast of Africa. Hurricanes typically form in August, September, or October when the ocean water is the warmest. With rising ocean water temperatures, we are seeing an increase in the severity of hurricanes.

### BOOKS TO DISPLAY

*Hurricane Watch* by Melissa Stewart. New York, NY: HarperCollins, 2015.

*If You Were a Kid Surviving a Hurricane* by Josh Gregory. New York, NY: Children's Press, 2018.

*Marvelous Cornelius: Hurricane Katrina and the Spirit of New Orleans* by Phil Bildner. San Francisco, CA: Chronicle Books, 2015.

*Survive a Hurricane* by Patrick Perish. Minneapolis, MN: Bellwether Media, 2017.

### DID YOU KNOW?

Short, distinctive names are given to tropical storms and hurricanes to avoid confusion. Prior to the 1950s, tropical storms and hurricanes were tracked by the year and order they occurred. However, there was often confusion when two or more tropical storms occurred at the same time. In 1953, the United States began using female names for storms. By 1978, both male and female names were used to identify Pacific storms and in 1979, they were used to identify storms in the Atlantic. The World Meteorological Organization regulates procedures for the naming of tropical storms. For Atlantic hurricanes, there is a list of male and female names that are used on a six-year rotation. If a storm is especially costly or deadly, that name is taken out of rotation. For example, Katrina was removed from the rotation after 2005. If there are more than 21 named tropical storms in a season, additional storms are named from the Greek alphabet.

## Hands-on Project

Hot air rising is an essential part of hurricanes formation. Using a light bulb, have participants watch how heat can cause air to rise.

### MATERIALS NEEDED

- 6" x 6" piece of construction paper per participant
- Scissors
- 4" piece of string
- Exposed light bulb to use as a heat source. Any lamp with the shade removed will work.

### DIRECTIONS

Have participants follow the instructions below

1. Cut the paper into a spiral, like a snail shell. For ease, use the pattern shown.

2. Tie a knot into one end of your string.

3. Poke a hole in the top of the paper spiral and pull the string through.

4. Turn on the light bulb.

5. Take turns holding their spirals above the light bulb.

6. What happens as the light bulb heats the air? Does the paper spin? Does the paper spin faster or slower depending on how close you are to the light bulb?

**LEARN MORE** Track tropical depressions, tropical storms, and hurricanes with the National Hurricane Center at **nhc.noaa.gov.** Storms in both the Atlantic and Pacific are tracked on this site, and charts containing public advisories, wind speed probabilities, warning cones maps, and more are available.

# Tornadoes

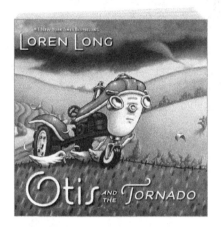

## *Otis and the Tornado*

Loren Long. New York, NY: Philomel Books, 2011.

Otis and his farm friends are enjoying a summer's day on the farm, except for the stubborn bull. When the weather turns ominous and the farmer runs for the cellar, Otis knows he needs to rescue the farm animals locked in the barn. Seeing a tornado heading toward the farm, Otis and the animals hide in a low area until Otis hears the bull bellowing. Otis makes the hard decision to help the bull before the tornado can reach them. Otis shows us that helping others is always important, and this book offers a good introduction to tornadoes for children.

### ABOUT TORNADOES

When warm, humid air rises from the ground toward a cumulonimbus thunderhead cloud, it creates an updraft that pulls warm, humid air with it. The air rises to where the temperature is cooler and condensation creates rain or hail. The cool air falls back toward the Earth, creating a downdraft. If the updraft and downdraft come together and start to spin, a funnel shaped cloud forms inside the thunderhead and sometimes tilts and reaches toward the ground. As the funnel spins faster, it sucks up more warm air and becomes bigger, louder, and more powerful. If it touches the ground, it becomes a tornado. The middle of the United States experiences tornadoes frequently and is often referred to as Tornado Alley. Most tornadoes occur in this area from April through June. Florida also has a higher number of tornadoes from January through March. There are more than 1,200 tornadoes per year in the United States, more than any other country. With global warming, we have more severe storms, which create conditions that are favorable for tornadoes to form.

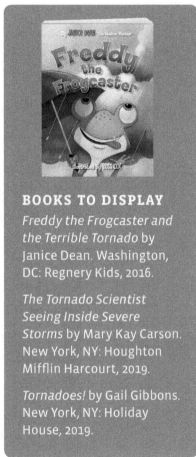

### BOOKS TO DISPLAY

*Freddy the Frogcaster and the Terrible Tornado* by Janice Dean. Washington, DC: Regnery Kids, 2016.

*The Tornado Scientist Seeing Inside Severe Storms* by Mary Kay Carson. New York, NY: Houghton Mifflin Harcourt, 2019.

*Tornadoes!* by Gail Gibbons. New York, NY: Holiday House, 2019.

## DID YOU KNOW?

In 1971, Dr. Tetsuya Theodore Fujita developed the Fujita Tornado Scale, rating tornadoes on a scale from F0 to F5. Since 2007, the Enhanced Fujita Tornado Scale has been used to classify tornadoes from EF0 to EF5. Classifications are based on the amount and type of damage caused. Most tornadoes occur in the afternoon and last less than ten minutes. Funnel clouds form over water too. When they touch down on water, they are called waterspouts.

# Hands-on Project

An easy way to demonstrate a tornado funnel is by making a tornado in a jar.

## MATERIALS NEEDED

- Several clear plastic jars or bottles with lids (enough for one per child)
- Water
- Dish soap
- Food coloring
- Assorted debris, such as small pieces of foil or glitter

## DIRECTIONS

Have participants follow the instructions below to create their own tornado in a jar.

1. Fill the jar three-fourths full with water.

2. Add 2 drops of dish soap.

3. Add 2 drops of food coloring.

4. Securely place on the lid.

5. Shake the jar upright and counterclockwise in a circular motion to observe a funnel formation.

6. Add the foil and other light items to demonstrate how a tornado picks up dirt and other debris and lifts them into its funnel.

Source: Rob Byron / Adobe Stock

**LEARN MORE** Through the millennia, there have been reports of raining frogs and fish. While that is obviously impossible, the strong winds of a tornado can suck up and lift animals and "rain" them elsewhere. The Library of Congress has an Everyday Mysteries site to help you get answers to many interesting questions through scientific inquiry by using their collections in science and technology. For more information on raining frogs and other mysteries, visit **loc.gov/rr/scitech/mysteries/rainingfrogs.html**.

# Earth Day

## *The Lorax*

Dr. Seuss. New York, NY: Random House, 1971.

A perfect introduction to the concept of environmental issues, this classic Dr. Seuss tale tells the story of a beautiful valley containing a forest of Truffula trees that support a variety of animals. The Truffula was known for its silk-like foliage and when the Once-ler discovered the trees, he chopped one down to knit a Thneed. The Once-ler is so excited by the money that can be made, he builds a factory to manufacture Thneeds. The Lorax, who speaks for the trees, warns repeatedly that this is a great mistake. Eventually the very last Truffula tree is cut, and the factory is forced to shut down. For years, the Once-ler ponders the message that the Lorax left for him in a pile of rocks: "UNLESS." When the Once-ler shares his story with a young boy living in the area, he finally realizes what the Lorax meant, "Unless someone like you cares a whole awful lot, nothing is going to get better. It's not." While news of climate change and environmental issues are prevalent, *The Lorax* reminds us that hope can come from the actions of just one person who uses their voice for change.

### ABOUT EARTH DAY

Before 1970, chemicals and smoke poured into the environment by manufacturing companies without regulation. Science and chemicals were seen as the solution to all issues, including pests, with little thought as to how they would affect ecosystems and nature. In 1969, after an oil spill in Santa Barbara, California, Senator Gaylord Nelson of Wisconsin organized a nationwide demonstration against pollution and in support of a more sustainable treatment of the environment. The protest was held on April 22, 1970, with approximately 20 million Americans participating across the country. Earth Day is observed annually around the world on April 22. The Earth Day Network now coordinates events globally in more than 193 countries.

---

**BOOKS TO DISPLAY**

*Green Queen* by Marci Peschke. North Mankato, MN: Capstone Picture Window Books, 2014.

*One Planet: The One Place We All Call Home* by Matt Whyman. London: HarperCollins Children's Books, 2019.

*Spring After Spring: How Rachel Carson Inspired the Environmental Movement* by Stephanie Roth Sisson. New York, NY: Roaring Brook Press, 2018.

*What Is Climate Change?* by Gail Herman. New York, NY: Penguin Random House, 2018.

### DID YOU KNOW?

Rachel Carson grew up in rural Pennsylvania with a deep appreciation of the natural world around her. In 1929, she received her undergraduate degree in Marine Biology and in 1932, she received her master's degree in Zoology from Johns Hopkins University. She worked as a scientist and became Editor-in-Chief of all publications for the U.S. Fish and Wildlife Service. After World War II, disturbed by the use of synthetic chemical pesticides, she spoke out about their profound effect on entire ecosystems. In 1962, Rachel Carson wrote the book *Silent Spring*, where she challenged these chemical practices and called for change. After the release of *Silent Spring*, President John F. Kennedy asked the Life Sciences Panel of the President's Science Advisory Committee to investigate her claims. Later, Rachel was called to testify at congressional hearings regarding chemical use. Following the investigation and Carson's testimony, Congress revised the regulation of chemicals. In 1976, the Toxic Substances Control Act was put in place, directing the Environmental Protection Agency to protect the public from unreasonable risk of injury to health and the environment from chemicals.

## Hands-on Project

Have participants use their imagination to create their own special Lorax garden.

### MATERIALS NEEDED

- Small repurposed containers
- Soil
- Succulents
- Moss or other small grass-like plants, which can be collected from a yard or wooded area that allows you to take plants
- Small ornamental objects like stones, gems, or miniature structures and animals
- Water

### DIRECTIONS

Have your participants follow the instructions below to make their own miniature Lorax garden.

1. Determine if your Lorax garden will be located inside or outside. This will help you determine the types of plants best for it.

2. Choose a container and add soil to it.

3. Using your imagination, what does your miniature garden look like? Begin adding plants.

4. Add other ornamental objects to the garden. Do you have a pathway of stones? Are there animals wandering among the plants?

5. Gently water the plants.

**LEARN MORE** For a variety of activities linked to the Lorax, visit Seussville at **seussville.com/Educators/lthe-lorax-project.**

CPSIA information can be obtained
at www.ICGtesting.com
Printed in the USA
LVHW020351140622
721151LV00007B/599

9 780838 947517